Don't Shriek, Maisie!

Published in the UK by Scholastic Education, 2022
Scholastic Distribution Centre, Bosworth Avenue, Tournament Fields, Warwick, CV34 6UQ
Scholastic Ireland, 89E Lagan Road, Dublin Industrial Estate, Glasnevin, Dublin, D11 HP5F

SCHOLASTIC and associated logos are trademarks and/or registered trademarks of Scholastic Inc.
www.scholastic.co.uk
© 2022 Scholastic
1 2 3 4 5 6 7 8 9   2 3 4 5 6 7 8 9 0 1

Printed by Ashford Colour Press
The book is made of materials from well-managed, FSC®-certified forests and other controlled sources.

A CIP catalogue record for this book is available from the British Library.

ISBN 978-0702-30914-4

All rights reserved. This book is sold subject to the condition that it shall not, by way of trade or otherwise, be lent, hired out or otherwise circulated in any form of binding or cover other than that in which it is published. No part of this publication may be reproduced, stored in a retrieval system, or transmitted in any form or by any other means (electronic, mechanical, photocopying, recording or otherwise) without prior written permission of Scholastic Limited.

Every effort has been made to trace copyright holders for the works reproduced in this publication, and the publishers apologise for any inadvertent omissions.

Author
Ann Hill
Editorial team
Rachel Morgan, Vicki Yates, Fiona Undrill, Jennie Clifford
Design team
Dipa Mistry, Justin Hoffmann, Andrea Lewis, We Are Grace
Illustrations
Christos Skaltsas/Advocate Art

Help your child to read!

This book practises these letters and letter sounds.
Point and say the sounds with your child:

- o (as in 'so')
- i (as 'kind')
- a (as in 'lazing')
- e (as in 'she')
- a-e (as in 'cave')
- i-e (as in 'bite')
- ie (as in 'Maisie')
- aw (as in 'lawn')

Your child may need help to read these common tricky words:

- the
- said
- are
- to
- have
- was
- of
- do
- you
- they
- little
- all
- put
- were
- when

Before reading
- Look at the cover picture and read the title together. Read the back cover blurb to your child.
- Ask your child: *Have you ever been afraid? What did you do?*

During reading
- If your child gets stuck on a word, remind them to sound it out and then blend the sounds to read the word: M-ai-s-ie, Maisie.
- If they are still stuck, show them how to read the word.
- Enjoy looking at the pictures together. Pause to talk about the story.

After reading
- Ask your child: *What did Maisie do that was brave? Why did she do it?*
- *Do you think Maisie will shriek when she sees a cat again? Why?*

Maisie didn't like picnics. She was afraid of bees, spiders and things with claws.

A cat was lazing on the lawn.
Mum said, "That cat is so cute."
But Maisie was afraid.

Next, a spider crawled across Maisie's plate.

Maisie shrieked!
"Don't shriek, Maisie. It won't bite!" said Dad.

Jade said, "Maisie, do you like snakes?"

The next day, they drove to the seaside. Jade played in the rock pools.

Maisie and Jade looked in a cave.
"Don't shriek, Maisie, but I can see a thing… with claws," said Jade.

Jade cried, "It's a little crab and it's all alone! We must put it in the sea."

"It has claws, so I might shriek," said Maisie. Jade sobbed, "Don't shriek, Maisie. Use the bucket to rescue it."

The crab crawled closer. Maisie felt... brave.

They put the crab in a pool.
Maisie said, "Poor crab. I think it was afraid, like me."

"You were brave and kind," said Mum. Dad gave Maisie and Jade a tub of strawberries.

Maisie didn't even mind when a spider peeped out ...and she didn't shriek!

Retell the story